I've Been Saved:
Now What!?

A Guide for New Believers

Guidance for those who have just begun their
faith journey.

Barry N. Key Jr.

Cover artwork by Austin Wilhite

ISBN: 979-8-218-86669-3
Printed in the United States of America

First Edition
First Printing 2025

Dedication

To my wife—
your faith, patience, and love helped guide me to the
Lord and have carried me through life ever since.

To the pastors—

who have faithfully guided me, challenged me, and
helped shape my walk with Christ.

To my children—
thank you for your grace as I learned to be a father.

And to friends and relatives who stood beside me along
the way—
your presence has meant more than words can say.

Most importantly to God—
who placed all these wonderful people in my life.

Foreword

It's my distinct joy and honor to write this foreword for my friend and brother in Christ, Pastor Barry Key, for his book I've Been Saved: Now What!? A Guide for New Believers.

I have had the privilege of knowing Barry for many years, and throughout that entire season, he has been a faithful servant of the Lord—teaching the Bible with clarity, living out his faith with humility, and modeling what it means to walk with Jesus daily. As a husband and father, Barry's life is a consistent reflection of the gospel he proclaims and is evidenced by his love for his sweet wife, Tracey, and his awesome son, Clay. As a firefighter, he has dedicated his life to protecting others, and as a believer, he has committed his heart to leading others toward eternal security in Christ, as is demonstrated by this wonderful resource.

It was my distinct honor to serve on Barry's ordination council as he was set apart for the gospel ministry—a moment that affirmed what so many of us already knew: his calling and character are genuine.

In I've Been Saved: Now What!?, Barry writes from the perspective of someone who has both studied the Word deeply and lived it out faithfully. What I appreciate about this book is that Barry's writing style is as engaging as it is insightful—he communicates deep biblical truths in a warm, practical, and enjoyable way that feels like a conversation with a trusted friend. My prayer is that new believers who read these pages will find not only direction for their next steps but also inspiration from the life of someone who walks the talk. I know it is Barry's heart, as it is mine, to see people who come to Christ find their spiritual footing in discipleship—and this is the perfect tool. It can be used individually, in a mentoring format, or even in a small-group setting.

I'm grateful for Pastor Barry Key's friendship, his ministry, and the impact this book will surely have in helping others grow in their walk with Jesus.

Pastor Rick Wright

Contents

Introduction

Proverbs 3:5-6

Trust in the Lord with all your heart, and lean not on your own understanding; In all your ways acknowledge Him, and He shall direct your paths.

Welcome

If you have a copy of this book in your hands, it's reasonable to assume that you've recently accepted Jesus Christ as your Lord and Savior. You either found this book in a search of some type or someone handed it to you after your profession of faith. Either way, I hope this book guides you as a new believer with the basic question of "where do I go from here?"

My beliefs

If you're new to the faith, it might help to know where I'm coming from—my personal beliefs about God and what it means to follow Him. Don't feel pressured to fully understand everything I'm about to share—unless something seems way off, just read on and take what helps. I'm laying these items out up front for several reasons. 1) If you are a new believer in a different denomination, where my thoughts may not line up with yours, you'll need to know up front. 2) If you are a pastor or friend looking for a book to give a new believer, this will quickly let you know if you can support it. 3) Trust in my writing; I want you as the reader to know where I am coming from with no hidden agenda.

I currently attend a Baptist church that is affiliated with the Southern Baptist Convention (SBC). I believe that Christ will return sometime in the future to call all believers to Himself, after which there will be a 7-year period of tribulation followed by a literal 1,000-year Kingdom here on Earth. This hope keeps me looking forward to and anticipating His return. These items classify me as a "Pretribulation (pretrib)–Premillennial (premil)" believer. The SBC recognizes other ways to view end times (Eschatology); these are just my views. I currently hold to a "Provisionist" view of salvation (Soteriology) which means – I believe that God provides sufficient grace for all humans and that we are free to accept or deny His provision for salvation. As with end times, there are several other views on soteriology; this is just my current view. For more mature believers I understand that the explanation of Provisionism is simplistic, but that is the point of this book.

With all of that said, don't get caught up in words like "eschatology" or "soteriology". They are fancy words that you will hear as you progress on your walk with Christ. In fact, your ideas on these items will probably change more than once as you grow and become more knowledgeable of God's Word. What do I mean when I say "your walk with Christ"? 1 John 2:6 says, "He who says he abides in Him ought himself also to walk just as He walked." Our "walk with Christ" is how we follow Him in our daily living. We are not perfect, as He is, but we strive to be that way. Growth on your walk is what believers refer to as sanctification. As you read and study the Bible, listen to sermons and teachers, you will grow deeper in your understanding and relationship to Jesus; this helps you grow as a believer and live more like He did. This growth is what people will notice as a change in you, we'll explore that change deeper in the chapter "What Has Changed".

How to use this book

Unless otherwise noted, all Scripture quotations are from the New King James Version (NKJV). Why the NKJV? Good question! I'll unpack that in the chapter 'How to Choose a Bible?'
Abbreviations of Scripture references:
- o New International Version (NIV)
- o English Standard Version (ESV)
- o New Living Translation (NLT)
- o New American Standard Version 1995 (NASB 1995)
- o The Message (MSG)

Scripture quotes vs. Scripture references. In writing this book I want to give you good solid information but at the same time I don't want to do all the work for you. Sometimes I'll quote Scripture directly. Other times, I'll just reference it. When a Scripture is referenced, think of it like a hyperlink on a web page; it's meant for you to click on and check out. I understand that not every new believer will have instant access to a Bible, but most will have their phone with them. Simply type the Scripture into your preferred search engine and it will bring the verse right to you. Try it now: Psalm 118:24 – and enjoy the day.

I use superscripts to differentiate between two types of notes: numbers (e.g., [1]) for bibliography references at the end of the book, and letters (e.g., [a]) for footnotes.

My goal is simple: short, sharp chapters that help you in each area. When I read a book, they look lived in—highlights, scribbles, notes in the margins. I want that for you here. There's space along the sides for your thoughts and a blank spot at each chapter's end for more notes. Grab a pen, dig in, mark it up—it's yours.

A note on quotes

I'll quote various people—pastors, writers, teachers—to shed light on key points. Quoting someone doesn't mean I endorse their full theology. For example, John Piper is a gifted teacher, but his Calvinist view of salvation differs from mine. I value his insight where it aligns with my understanding of Scripture, not where it leans into what I'd call 'Calvinistic' territory—my term, not his. My aim is to use what helps you grow, drawing only on what aligns with God's Word as I understand it.

Trust but verify

In Acts 17:10-15 Paul and Silas travel to a town called Berea. The people of the town listened eagerly to the teachings, but after listening they "searched the Scriptures daily *to find out* whether these things were so." (Acts 17:11) The people of Berea would fact check

Paul! I promise you I am no Paul–fact check me, please. Look up my Scripture references, check the books and web pages I quote. I've read books that made it through professional publishers and still ended up with mistakes when they came to print. Please follow up especially if it's something you disagree with. Try it now: type in or look up Acts 17:10-15 and read the story.

For mature believers

A note to mature believers who may be reading this book. I kindly ask for some grace as you read through the chapters. This book is written intentionally simplistic. It is milk for new believers and not intended as a great theological treatise. If you're from a non-Baptist background, please know that nothing in this book is intended to offend; some differences may be mentioned only for clarification. If you are a Baptist, please remember this is written to a larger audience and I do my best to offer other basic theological views that don't violate Christian essentials. An example of this is Baptism, where we, as Baptists, hold to full submersion of professed believers; R. C. Sproul (1992)[1] writes: "The command to baptize may be fulfilled by immersion, dipping, or sprinkling." Though I hold to submersion, pointing out his view does not violate essential beliefs.

With all of that said, are you ready to begin your walk ... let's go.

Chapter 1

First Question

Romans 10:9

that if you confess with your mouth the Lord Jesus and believe in your heart that God has raised Him from the dead, you will be saved.

Was I truly saved?

I remember lying in bed in Maracaibo, Venezuela, tossing and turning because of the strong pull on my heart. Why Venezuela? That story is in another chapter near the end of the book; nevertheless, I was lying there with my heart being torn apart when I finally gave in, rolled out of bed, hit my knees, and gave my life to Christ.

You probably felt a similar tug before you responded to the call to follow Jesus. A strong pull, an undeniable draw, an unquenchable desire to go down front, raise your hand, hit your knees. Whatever it was, you just had to do it – and you did. The question now becomes, "Was it an emotional response to what was happening around me or was it true heartfelt surrender to Christ?" The answer is: only you and God know. No one around you, not your friends, your parents, your pastor, no one else, is able to see your heart except for God. God may know for sure, but how do you?

2 Corinthians 13:5a says, "Examine yourselves *as to* whether you are in the faith. Test yourselves." So how do we examine and test ourselves to know that we are in the faith? Here are a few ways:

1. Have you believed and confessed the Gospel? 1 Corinthians 15:3-4 says, "For I delivered to you first of all that which I also received: that Christ died for our sins according to the Scriptures, and that He was buried, and that He rose again the third day according to the Scriptures," then Romans 10:9 says "that if you confess with your mouth the Lord Jesus and believe in your heart that God has raised Him from the dead, you will be saved." So, do you truly believe that Jesus died for your sins, was buried, and rose on the third day and have you confessed that belief? If so, then you have been saved.

2. Have you repented of your sins? Before answering this question, you need to know what repentance is. The literal translation is "to change one's mind", but that would be an oversimplification of the meaning. A closer definition would be "a change of mind that results in a change of action[1]". For the purposes of this book think of it like this: in order to believe the Gospel, you had to admit that you were a sinner in need of salvation (Romans 3:23). Once you believed and confessed the Gospel, then you confess and turn from the sins that caused you to be in need of salvation[a]. Think of this turning as a 180-degree about face and going in the opposite

2

direction. If you were running towards a house and noticed a time bomb on the porch counting down and it was close to zero, you would immediately turn around and run as hard and fast as you could in the opposite direction; that is repentance of sins.

3. Do you have a desire to read, understand and obey God's word? 2 Timothy 3:16-17 says, "All Scripture is given by inspiration of God, and is profitable for doctrine, for reproof, for correction, for instruction in righteousness, that the man of God may be complete, thoroughly equipped for every good work." What do those verses mean? Matthew Henry puts it this way, "it is profitable for all purposes of the Christian life."[2] How-to books sell millions of copies every year, think of the Bible as a how-to book for living the Christian life. I once heard a pastor say, "the answer to every question is not in the Bible, but the answer to every question needed for salvation and sanctification is." In other words, how many planets are in the solar system is not answered, but how one comes to the knowledge of salvation is. The Bible can be hard to understand, especially in the beginning. Even the apostle Peter found some of Paul's writings hard. In 2 Peter 3:15-16, he says, "as also our beloved brother Paul, according to the wisdom given to him, has written to you, as also in all his epistles, speaking in them of these things, in which are some things hard to understand,". The desire for God's word should direct you to want to read and understand the

Bible to the best of your ability. I devote an entire chapter to choosing a Bible version that is best for you.

4. You will want to share what Jesus has done for you. When you are saved there is a desire in your heart to spread that knowledge to others. There is a joy you feel that you will want to explain to everyone who will listen, but the words will fall short. As you mature in your belief your ability to share the Gospel will improve and you will be able to tell your story (testimony). I have been saved for over 15 years now and if I share my story with a group, I still get tears in my eyes. We will explore your testimony in the chapter "Be Ready with Your Story".

This is not an exhaustive list, but if these four things have happened and are present in your life, it's safe to say that you have been saved.

With that said, how can you have assurance? 1 John 5:11-13 (NLT) "And this is what God has testified: He has given us eternal life, and this life is in his Son. Whoever has the Son has life; whoever does not have God's Son does not have life. I have written this to you who believe in the name of the Son of God, so that *you may know you have eternal life*." (Italics mine) John tells us that we can "know" that we have eternal life. Every believer I have ever met has doubts every now and then. This is normal, but we do not live in those doubts. If you catch yourself doubting, think of this: people that are not saved have no reason to doubt their salvation. During these times dive deeper into the word, talk to a mentor or another believer.

In reading the things above you should have noticed something, they all indicate a change. Let's step into the next chapter and see "What has changed"?

Footnote

a. In trying to cover only the basics in this book there are subjects that can't be fully explored, repentance is one of them. It is a deep subject that includes your daily walk (Luke 9:23). As you progress on your walk dive deeper into this subject through study and discussions with more mature believers.

Notes

Notes

Chapter 2

What has Changed?

2 Corinthians 5:17

Therefore, if anyone is in Christ, he is a new creation; old things have passed away; behold, all things have become new.

There's an old Joe Walsh[1] song that says, "Everybody's so different, I haven't changed." He describes in the song how when he became famous everybody around him started acting differently but that he hadn't changed. As a new believer, you will notice that people will begin to act differently around you, but **you** have changed.

You've now confessed Jesus Christ as your Lord and Savior— what has changed? In a sense nothing changed and in a sense everything changed. When you look in the mirror you are still you. Same haircut, same eye color, same weight, same old you. 2 Corinthians 5:17 says "Therefore, if anyone is in Christ, he is a new creation; old things have passed away; behold, all things have become new." If all you see is the "old you" how are you a "new creation"?

Becoming a 'new you' doesn't always look the same. For some, it's a dramatic 180-degree shift. For others, it's a gradual transformation over time. Where the individual is in life, what they have been through and what has brought them to this point affects that change.

For instance, someone who has had a rough life and is addicted to drugs or alcohol may have a complete change. They may set aside whatever the addiction is and never touch it again. We hear these stories often; their family and friends can't believe the change that happened. On the other end of the spectrum is that person who was raised in a "Christian" home. They have a good family, good friends, and a nice middle-class life. They might have even called themselves a Christian if you asked. When this person comes to true faith, the change at first, may be almost imperceptible. They may start attending a church more frequently, their language may start to change, or they may start talking more openly about Jesus and the Bible. Both of these individuals were changed by Christ, but the immediate outward change appears different. Please do not judge your change against someone else's. The point is this: the depth of your change isn't measured by how visible it is to others. What matters is that it's real.

Peter was a simple fisherman who was called to follow Jesus early in Jesus' ministry. As you read through the Gospels, you will see there was definitely a slow change over time for Peter. He questions, he makes mistakes and at times just doesn't get it; but eventually he grows into the Apostle Peter no longer the simple fisherman.

Then there is Paul. Paul was a persecutor of Christians. At the beginning of Acts 9 Paul is asking for permission to arrest Christians in Damascus. Acts 9:1-2 says, "Then

Saul, still breathing threats and murder against the disciples of the Lord, went to the high priest and asked letters from him to the synagogues of Damascus, so that if he found any who were of the Way[a], whether men or women, he might bring them bound to Jerusalem." The Lord had other plans for him as you read on, Acts 9:3-6 says, "As he journeyed he came near Damascus, and suddenly a light shone around him from heaven. Then he fell to the ground, and heard a voice saying to him, "Saul, Saul[b], why are you persecuting Me?" And he said, "Who are You, Lord?" Then the Lord said, "I am Jesus, whom you are persecuting. It is hard for you to kick against the goads." So he, trembling and astonished, said, "Lord, what do You want me to do?" Paul in an instant changed.

Can you say Peter was better than Paul—or Paul better than Peter? Of course not. Each had a personal and legitimate encounter with the Lord, and both were changed from the inside out. Your experience may be different, but it's no less real. You probably didn't have a flash of blinding light knock you to the ground, but your encounter with Jesus is just as valid as Paul's.

Now that you've begun this journey with Jesus, what comes next? How do you grow in this new life? One of the best things you can do is connect in fellowship with other believers. God never meant for us to walk this road alone. Surrounding yourself with a healthy, Bible-believing church will help you grow, encourage you when things get tough, and keep you grounded in truth. So, let's talk about that—how do you find a good church?

Footnotes

a. "who were of the Way" – this is how followers of Christ were often referred to before they were actually called "Christians". This happens in the book of Acts 11:26 "And when he had found him, he brought him to Antioch. So it was that for a whole year they assembled with the church and taught a great many people. And the disciples were first called Christians in Antioch."

b. "Saul" – for new believers Paul actually had 2 names. He was Jewish (a Hebrew) and a Roman citizen. Saul was his Hebrew name and Paul was his Roman name.

Notes

Chapter 3
Find a Good Church

Hebrews 10:24-25

And let us consider one another in order to stir up love and good works, not forsaking the assembling of ourselves together, as is the manner of some, but exhorting one another, and so much the more as you see the Day approaching.

If you professed faith at a church you were visiting or at an event, such as a concert, the first step on your journey should be to find a good Bible teaching church. While looking for a church, remember the old adage, "if you find a perfect church, don't join it because you will only mess it up." The perfect church does not exist. Churches are not full of perfect people worshipping a fallible God; they are full of fallible people worshipping an infallible God. With that said, if you walk into a church for the first time and are treated in an unfriendly manner, go ahead and move on down the road. Your first visit should feel warm and welcoming. Hopefully through the next few paragraphs I will be able to give you helpful advice on how to find the right church for you.

The first thing you will want to think of is distance. The church you attend doesn't need to be next door, but it does need to be close enough that you will not be tempted to use the distance as an excuse to not go. If you get plugged into a good church and want to fellowship and serve, you will need to be close enough that it's easily accessible. My church is only 8-10 minutes up the road, but we have people that travel up to 45 minutes to get there. Just to see, I opened Google Maps, put a pin on my house, and searched for churches. There are literally three dozen plus churches within a 20–30-minute drive. I live deep in the Bible Belt; you may not have this luxury.

Once you have decided how far you are willing to travel, research the churches within that distance. Ask friends or neighbors that attend church where they go and what their beliefs are. If you feel drawn to one denomination or another, look for those churches within that distance. If you don't initially have a preference look up all of the churches in your area and see if they have websites. Often churches will have their statements of faith online so you can see what they believe or what their style of worship is. If you are unsure, do an internet search of the denomination you are looking at and see what their beliefs are. The most important thing you will want to find, no matter the distance, is a church that teaches sound doctrine directly from the Bible.

So, what do I mean when I say "sound doctrine directly from the Bible?" Different churches and pastors teach in different styles but they should all teach directly from the Word of God and not from their own ideals. There are pastors who teach verse by verse through books of the Bible. Instead of teaching specific topics or applications, they teach each verse and let the topics or applications come organically from the text. There are pastors who teach topically. They will take topics like grace, salvation, or forgiveness and teach an entire lesson from the different verses that touch on the topic. The previous pastor of our church enjoyed mixing the styles. He would teach a verse-by-verse study through a book and when that was complete, he would do several sermons on topics and then return for another verse by verse through another book. Any of these styles are ok as long as what they are teaching is straight from the Bible. If you visit a church and they have materials they teach from that are above the Bible or on the same level as the Bible, you will want to visit another church. Examples of this would be:

- The Church of Jesus Christ of Latter-day Saints (LDS Church): they believe that the Book of Mormon and the Bible are both the Word of God. According to the church's "Articles of Faith"—a document written by Joseph Smith in 1842 and canonized by the church as Scripture in 1880—members "believe the Bible to be the word of God as far as it is translated correctly,"; and they "believe the Book of Mormon to be the word of God," without qualification.[1]

- Christian Science: Science and Health with Key to the Scriptures by Mary Baker Eddy. They view this text as equal to the Bible. "For Christian Scientists, Science and Health is not merely a commentary but a divinely inspired text that reveals the spiritual laws of God, making it equal in authority to the Bible within their theology"[2].

13

The Bible clearly states in Revelation 22:18–19, "For I testify to everyone who hears the words of the prophecy of this book: If anyone adds to these things, God will add to him the plagues that are written in this book; and if anyone takes away from the words of the book of this prophecy, God shall take away his part from the Book of Life, from the holy city, and from the things which are written in this book." Remember these verses if you visit a church that wants to add to the Bible. You can also look up Deuteronomy 4:2 and Deuteronomy 12:32 for further reference.

If you have children, check what kind of youth or children's ministry the church offers. Are the teachers friendly and attentive? Is it safe? Are the lessons biblical and age-appropriate? Ask to sit in on a class or review the materials. Is it just babysitting, or are they actually teaching the Word? Proverbs 22:6 says, "Train up a child in the way he should go, and when he is old he will not depart from it". It's vital that your kids grow in their understanding, too.

Note a church's fellowship opportunities. Do the people in the church fellowship together at times other than Sunday morning? Are there small groups? Some churches have what are called small groups that gather, usually at someone's home, at times other than during church. These groups are made up of various types of people. There are men's groups, women's groups, teen groups, couples' groups, etc. Groups can be based on anything that draws people together in fellowship and study of the Lord. I knew of one group that gathered together at an indoor firing range. The range had an eating area where they would gather, have devotion, prayer and then they would go out to the range and have a good time together. At the church I currently attend, our small groups gather to discuss the previous sermon from our pastor. I should phrase that in another way; we gather to discuss and dive deeper into the subject and/or verses that our pastor discussed during his sermon. As I write this, my small group consists of a single guy in his 20's, a single lady, a young couple without children, two couples each with 2 children at home and 2 couples that are "mature" and have grandchildren. It is an eclectic mix of people but it's awesome. Most churches that have small groups will have some way of learning about the groups offered. Whether online or in the lobby, check out the groups and find one and visit them.

Since you are new to the faith, another consideration is, do they have Sunday school classes? Some churches have Sunday school classes, some have small groups and some have both. The church I attend has both. We have 2 adult classes on Sundays prior to our main service. There are classes for children and youth also. If you are new, I highly recommend finding a church with a good Sunday school program. Sermons are fantastic but it's hard to raise your hand and ask questions about a topic or verse you don't understand, this is where Sunday school comes in. Our class has 4 teachers and we rotate each week. The four of us teach in different styles but have the same theory during class: ask questions! We encourage questions and open discussion during class. One of the things I like about all four of us is that we are not afraid to say, "I don't know". My response to a question that I don't know is usually, "I honestly don't have an answer to that, but I will look into it this week and get back with you next week." Another thing we each do well is to inform the students when we are giving our understanding of a certain verse or topic. There are topics in the Bible that even the greatest biblical scholars of history disagree on. When I teach one of these subjects, I always preface the teaching with "this is Barry's understanding of the Scriptures". I do my best to offer the facts on both sides but I do think the class deserves to know where I stand.

I want to preface this next point with: the priority in attending church is to worship and learn about God and His word. Keep that in mind when I say that another thing to look for is the style of worship music. We are not there for the "show" or for a "concert," but if the style of music distracts you, that may not be the place for you. Different churches and different denominations conduct worship in various ways. There are denominations that allow no musical instruments at all, only "a cappella" singing is allowed. Other denominations have a broad spectrum from only non-electrical instruments to full worship bands. Some only sing hymns from their chosen hymnal, some use contemporary Christian music and others mix and match. Find what works for you, but don't let the music style be what keeps you at a church. I don't care how much you like the music, if the preaching and teaching are not sound, move on.

How open is the church with its finances? My church has a meeting of the members each year to approve the budget for the upcoming year. A copy of the proposed budget is handed out weeks prior to the meeting.

Members are allowed to see where the money is going and to ask questions about how it is being spent. Each quarter, our pastor sends an update showing our financial status. At any time a member wishes, they can ask to see the financial records to know where the money is being spent. We hide nothing; it is all in the open for everyone to see. If you begin attending a church and you find they are secretive about where some or all of the money is spent, at the very least be suspicious. In the end, you will probably want to find a different church.

When I began writing this book, I didn't realize this chapter would become one of the longest. But as I wrote, it became clear: one of the most important decisions you'll make as a new believer is where you attend church. This choice will shape your spiritual foundation—and your family's. How you grow in faith, knowledge, and understanding will be deeply influenced by it. Please don't take it lightly.

On the bibliography page, I've included QR codes linking to church locator tools. These can help you begin your search, but ultimately, visit the churches. Speak with the leaders. Talk with the members. Find a place where you can worship, grow, and walk securely in your faith.

If you were saved at a church you already attend or plan to attend, baptism has probably already been discussed with you. If not, then the next step is baptism. Turn the page—and let's step into the water.

Notes

Chapter 4

Baptism

Romans 6:3-4

Or do you not know that as many of us as were baptized into Christ Jesus were baptized into His death? Therefore we were buried with Him through baptism into death, that just as Christ was raised from the dead by the glory of the Father, even so we also should walk in newness of life.

The questions asked about baptism are: What is it? Should I do it? How should I do it? When should I do it? Who should do it?

What is it?

Let's start with what it is. From GotQuestions.org[1], "Very simply, water baptism is an outward testimony of the inward change in a believer's life. It illustrates a believer's identification with Christ's death, burial, and resurrection." Baptism is how we openly profess that we are now Christians. Almost all Protestant denominations or churches hold to some form of baptism and its necessity. Here are a few examples of what different churches believe about baptism:

Baptist: baptism is for professing believers; it is not required for salvation, but is a very important step in obedience to Christ; it is a symbolic representation of being buried and raised to new life as Christ was, it should be done by full immersion

Church of Christ: baptism is required for salvation; should be done as soon as possible, preferably right then, if possible; should be done by full immersion; baptism is required for entry into the church.

Methodist: they see baptism as a profound sign of God's love, a visible sign of inward change, and a vital step in the journey of Christian discipleship. Modes – immersion, pouring, or sprinkling – are not considered theologically significant, as long as water is used and the person is baptized in the name of the Father, Son, and Holy Spirit: infants and children can be baptized and baptism is a one-time only event.

Please remember these are simplistic and basic views, solely for this book. For more information on the different doctrines, I recommend doing some research on the church you have chosen to attend. Online sources can also offer help. I highly recommend the YouTube channel Ready to Harvest[2]. They do an excellent job of presenting different church's doctrines without added commentary, just straightforward facts.

Should you?

Churches may differ on some points of baptism, but the vast majority agree on the "you should" part. Baptism is considered by most Protestants as one of two ordinances. An ordinance is a divinely ordained ceremony or ritual, established by Jesus, that is observed by the church. The two normally recognized are baptism and communion (the Lord's Supper).

- Matthew 28:18-20 says, "And Jesus came and spoke to them, saying, "All authority has been given to Me in heaven and on earth. Go therefore and make disciples of all the nations, baptizing them in the name of the Father and of the Son and of the Holy Spirit, teaching them to observe all things that I have commanded you; and lo, I am with you always, even to the end of the age." Amen."

- 1 Corinthians 11: 23-26 "For I received from the Lord that which I also delivered to you: that the Lord Jesus on the same night in which He was betrayed took bread; and when He had given thanks, He broke it and said, "Take, eat; this is My body which is broken for you; do this in remembrance of Me." In the same manner He also took the cup after supper, saying, "This cup is the new covenant in My blood. This do, as often as you drink it, in remembrance of Me." For as often as you eat this bread and drink this cup, you proclaim the Lord's death till He comes."

If these are instituted and ordained by Jesus then it follows that to be in obedience to Him, we would want to participate in both. Since it is ordained by Christ the view of most churches is that it is not optional and should be done.

When Should You?

You now know what baptism is and that you should do it. So the next question is: when? Churches are all over the books on this issue. Some churches say right then, they will baptize you before you ever leave the building. Others may not say immediately but there is urgency to it. Still others, such as the church I was baptized in, will want to walk with the new believer and disciple them for a while before baptizing them. The church I currently attend will baptize you as quickly as you would like. We normally conduct baptism and communion the first Sunday of every month, however, our pastor will baptize you that day if you wish. We emphasize that there should be a desire by the believer to be baptized, but that the individual should follow Christ as quickly as they feel led.

How Should You?

By what mode or form should you be baptized? Being Southern Baptist I will always recommend full immersion unless you are physically limited and unable to do it that way. Wayne Grudem in Systematic Theology states, "The Greek word *baptizō* means, 'to plunge, dip, immerse' something in water. This is the commonly recognized and standard meaning of the term in ancient Greek literature both inside and outside of the Bible."[3] However, in his book Essential Truths of the Christian Faith, R. C. Sproul says, "Baptism signifies a washing with water. The command to baptize may be fulfilled by immersion, dipping, or sprinkling. The Greek word *to baptize* includes all three possibilities."[4] If the church you attend only suggests sprinkling, then follow your church's doctrine. I would like to point out, if you are unsure, full immersion should be acceptable to all churches.

Who Should?

Who should be baptized? Continuing to follow my roots, I believe that all professing Christians should be baptized. I believe this would be true of almost all denominations, if you believe, you should be baptized at some point in your life. Whether or not to baptize infants and children is a debate that has gone on for centuries. I am nowhere near qualified to jump into a debate on whether Acts 16:33 "And immediately he and all his family were baptized." included infants or not. I will say that every time I see baptism in the Bible it is of someone who has just professed faith. My opinion is that baptism is for professing Christians that are able to understand the commitment they have entered into and the reasons for which they are being baptized. That is simply my opinion, please follow the doctrine of the church you have chosen to attend. My biggest piece of advice is, if you are unsure then get baptized.

Clarification of Protestant

I would like to inject a point of clarification here; I used the word Protestant and realized as a new believer you may not know what that means. Without going too deep, a Protestant is basically anyone outside of Catholicism or Orthodox churches. I differentiate Protestant because

Catholic and Orthodox churches recognize baptism and communion as two of the up to seven sacraments. I won't go any deeper in this book than to say that ordinances and sacraments are viewed differently. As with other doctrines in this book, if this piques your interest then please do some deeper research. You may start with TheGospelCoalition.com for a protestant view or Catholic.com for a Catholic perspective.

Now that you understand baptism is important and that you should probably participate in it, the next question you may be asking is: what comes next in my walk? One of the best places to start is by reading the Bible—but with so many different translations available, how do you choose the right one? Let's take a look at how to pick a Bible that's trustworthy, readable, and helpful for your journey with Christ.

Notes

Chapter 5

How to Choose a Bible

Psalm 119:105

Your word is a lamp to my feet and a light to my path.

"Walk into a bookstore or scroll online, and you'll see Bibles everywhere—King James, New King James, NIV, ESV, NLT, and more. Why so many? Is one better than the others? And the big question: "Which is right for me?"

I believe in the inerrancy of the Bible as it was written in its original inspired form. 2 Timothy 3:16 says: "All Scripture is given by inspiration of God, and is profitable for doctrine, for reproof, for correction, for instruction in righteousness," this is one of Scripture's bedrock verses. You can find similar thoughts in 1 Thessalonians 2:13, Matthew 24:35, and others. In other words, I believe that when Paul wrote 2 Timothy he did so by the inspiration of the Holy Spirit, and that what he wrote was the inerrant Word of God.

But if it is God's Word and inerrant, why all these versions? Tons of books have been written about Bible translations. To keep this book short and on a basic level I'll try to make it as simple as I can. Translations are produced from documents that are 1000s of years old called manuscripts. There are several manuscript traditions that different translations rely on. After a Bible translation team decides which line of manuscripts to follow, they then decide which approach they wish to use. In other words, do they want to be a more literal word-for-word translation or more of a thought-for-thought translation. Here is an example of the difference:

- NASB 1995 (Hebrews 1:1-2): "God, after He spoke long ago to the fathers in many portions and in many ways in the prophets, has in these last days spoken to us by His Son, whom He has appointed heir of all things, through whom also He made the world."
- NLT (Hebrews 1:1-2): "Long ago God spoke to our ancestors through the prophets at many times and in many ways. But now in these final days, he has spoken to us through his Son. God has made the Son heir of everything, and through the Son, he created the universe."

Some translations even go to the point of being paraphrases instead of an actual translation. Here are those same two verses from The Message:

- MSG (Hebrews 1:1-2): "Going through a long line of prophets, God has been addressing our ancestors in different ways for centuries. Recently he spoke to us directly through his Son. By his Son, God created the world in the beginning, and it will all belong to the Son at the end."

Another reason there are numerous translations is that different teams translate words differently, not wrongly,

26

but differently. The original New Testament was written in Greek, more specifically Koine (coin-a) Greek. Greek words can have multiple meanings when translated into English—and the same is true in reverse. An example of an English word that would have multiple words in Greek is love. In Koine Greek, there were four distinct words for love depending on what was being stated: eros, philia, storge (not in the Bible), and agape. An example of a Greek word being translated differently would be epithumia in Galatians 5:17. The NKJV translates it 'lusts,' while the NIV uses 'desires.' Both are correct; the translation teams just pick the word that flows best with their style.

So which Bible translation is right for you? Well, that depends on a few factors. According to Pastor Mike Winger[1], two factors you should consider are, education level and reading comprehension. If you are completely new to reading the Bible, you may want to start with something along the lines of the NLT. It is a borderline paraphrase rather than a strict translation, but it is solid and gets the main points across. If you are more advanced in reading, then you may want to choose along the lines of the NKJV or the NIV. These are between word for word and thought for thought translations. If you really want to dig deep, try the ESV or the NASB. These are 2 of the most literal translations and are good for deep study.

As I stated in the introduction of the book, I mostly use the NKJV. The reason? The pastor at the church where I was baptized taught and preached from it. I bought one to follow along and have just stuck with it. I teach a

Sunday school class and most of the people in the class also use the NKJV. However, at home for study I will have several versions open, my go-to's are NASB 1995, NKJV, NIV and NLT. There are other study materials I use but that's for a different book.

Are there versions I avoid? Yes. Take the New World Translation (NWT). It is the translation used by Jehovah's Witnesses. This translation down plays, avoids or denies the deity of Christ. The most famous example is John 1:1

- NKJV: In the beginning was the Word, and the Word was with God, and the Word was God.
- NWT: In the beginning was the Word, and the Word was with God, and the Word was *a god*. (emphasis mine)

Another example is the Passion "Translation". Pastor Mike Winger has several videos on YouTube about this translation and why it is bad. If you are thinking about this one because someone recommended it, please watch at least one of those videos first. My advice is to stick with a mainline translation until you are more versed (pun intended) in the Bible.

Another consideration for choosing a Bible is which format of the translation should you choose? The broad spectrum of a Bible is the translation, such as The New King James Version. The NKJV, like most translations, comes in many different formats such as study Bibles, large print, journaling Bibles, etc. ... As a new believer I would recommend you start with a good study Bible of whichever translation you choose. Study Bibles have notes on verses, parallel passage references, some have maps, timelines, reading plans and other helpful chapters. Almost all of the major translations will have study versions. My personal Bible is a Journaling Bible. It has wide lined margins where I can take notes during sermons or classes. This helps me in future studies; I don't have to dig out notes, they are right there on the pages. Also consider size. Some of the study Bibles can be quite large. These are good for home study but not so good for carrying to Sunday school or church.

Wrapping this chapter up, in the beginning of your walk, choose a good solid translation that is easy for you to read, easy for you to take with you and helps bring God's Word alive for you. Once you've chosen a Bible, how do you read and study it? Move to the next chapter and find out.

Notes

Notes

Chapter 6
How to Study the Bible

Joshua 1:8

This Book of the Law shall not depart from your mouth, but you shall meditate in it day and night, that you may observe to do according to all that is written in it. For then you will make your way prosperous, and then you will have good success.

In the chapter from which the above verse is taken, God is commissioning Joshua to be the new leader of Israel. For context, especially for the new believer, "this Book of the Law" refers to God's written Word. So God is telling Joshua to read the word, study the word, and live by the word. If he does these things, he will prosper in God's ways. God affirms these principles through Paul when he writes to Timothy. 2 Timothy 3:16–17 says, "All Scripture is given by inspiration of God, and is profitable for doctrine, for reproof, for correction, for instruction in righteousness, that the man of God may be complete, thoroughly equipped for every good work." Our takeaway from this should be that we need to read the Word, study the Word, and live the Word.

In the beginning, take time to simply read the Bible. If this is your first time reading the Bible, take note that it is not a "book" itself. It is a collection of 66 books divided into two broad sections which are called the Old Testament (39 books) and the New Testament (27 books). As a new believer, nothing says you have to start with Genesis 1:1 and read straight through to Revelation 22:21. As a matter of fact, not many believers I know have ever done this. Start with the One in whom you've placed your faith—Jesus Christ. The first four books of the New Testament are called the Gospels. The word Gospel means good news; therefore, these four books are the good news of Jesus Christ. They explain to us who He was, why He came, and why He had to die. Pick one of these four books and dive in. A lot of scholars suggest that you start with the book of John. John's Gospel emphasizes the divinity of Jesus, meaning He is God. John's writing is straightforward and focused, and it helps strengthen your relationship with Jesus by highlighting His love, compassion and willingness to save. Set aside a little time each day to just sit and read. I once heard someone say there are two ways to read the Bible, leaning forward and leaning back. The kind of reading I'm referring to here is 'leaning back' reading. Open the book, lean back, and just enjoy it. Don't dig in, mark, highlight or follow references; just absorb it. After you have been leaning back and reading for a while you'll reach a point where you will want to go deeper. This is where leaning in begins.

One simple and effective way to begin studying the Bible is called the **SOAP** method. SOAP stands for Scripture, Observation, Application, and Prayer. This method gives you a practical way to dig into God's Word without needing a theology degree or a pile of study tools. Here's how it works:

S – Scripture

Start by picking a passage of Scripture–this could be a few verses, a short paragraph, or even a whole chapter if you have the time. Write down the specific verse or passage that stands out to you. For example, if you're reading John 15 and verse 5 jumps out, you'd write:

"I am the vine, you are the branches. He who abides in Me, and I in him, bears much fruit; for without Me you can do nothing." (John 15:5)

O – Observation

Next, take a few minutes to observe what the verse is saying. What's going on in the passage? Who is speaking? Who is being spoken to? Is there a command, a promise, a warning, or an encouragement? Write down your observations, even if they seem simple.

Jesus is describing a relationship between Himself and His followers. He's saying we need to stay connected to Him in order to bear fruit.

A – Application

Now bring it home. How does this verse apply to your life? What is God showing you personally? Is there something you need to change, remember, or do differently because of what you read?

I've been trying to do things in my own strength lately. This verse reminds me that I need to stay spiritually connected to Jesus in order to live a fruitful life.

P – Prayer

Close your time with a short prayer based on what you've read and learned. It doesn't have to be long or fancy—just honest. Ask the Holy Spirit to help you apply what you've learned.
Lord, help me stay connected to You today. Remind me that without You, I can do nothing. Thank You for always being nearby. Amen.

This simple method can turn a short daily reading into something meaningful that sticks with you throughout the day. All you need is a Bible, a notebook, and a few quiet minutes.

This chapter is meant to serve as a helpful starting point for new believers. The tools and approaches shared here, like simply reading the Word and using the SOAP method, are easy and effective for beginners. However, as you grow in your faith and understanding, you'll likely reach a point where you'll want to go deeper. When that happens, don't hesitate to explore additional resources—commentaries, interlinear Bibles, online classes or even college-level courses—that can help you dive further into God's Word and apply it more fully to your life. Growth is a lifelong journey, and every step you take in the Word brings you closer to knowing God more intimately. I will list a few other resources and pastors that I have found to be trustworthy on the bibliography page. These can help as you decide to go deeper.

In the study method above, we closed each study session with prayer. In the next chapter we will discuss what prayer is and what it isn't.

Notes

Notes

Chapter 7

Prayer

Colossians 4:2

Continue earnestly in prayer, being vigilant in it with thanksgiving;

As a new believer, you may have some misconceptions of what prayer is and what it is for. Here are some common misunderstandings about prayer. This list isn't exhaustive, but it covers the basics.

Prayer is not:
- Asking a genie in the sky for your wishes to come true
- Convincing God that you are right and He is wrong about a subject
- Twisting God's arm to see your point of view
- Chanting or mantras (words repeated over and over again)

Prayer is also simpler than you think—you don't need to be:
- An eloquent speaker
- A pastor, elder, or deacon to pray for someone
- In any specific position (lying face down, kneeling, hands folded, etc…)
- In a specific place (church, quiet room, altar)

So then, what is prayer? At its most basic level prayer is communication. Think of it in the context of a relationship. If you are in a committed relationship, married, dating or just starting to get to know someone; how well will that relationship grow if you don't speak to each other? You can read every self-help book ever written about relationships but if you don't communicate, it won't work. The same holds true for your relationship with God. Your time in prayer is your communication with God. Thank Him for what He's done for you, ask Him for your needs, apologize for what you've done wrong; you know, just talk with Him.

The next question is usually, if God is "all knowing" then why doesn't He just give me those things? When I'm teaching about prayer in Sunday school, I teach it like this: "when our son came to live with us, he was young and had very few words. Sitting at the kitchen table he would often point at something, like the butter dish, and grunt. We knew exactly what he wanted and that eventually we would give it to him, but for his growth and improvement we would make him "use his words."" The same holds true for prayer, yes God knows what you want but more importantly He knows what you need. To grow your faith, He wants you to "use your words." James 4:2 says, "Yet you do not have because you do not ask." Just as we helped our son grow by asking him to use his words, God asks us to "use our words".

That's why we pray, let's now discuss the how-to part. How to pray depends on many variables: why are you praying (conversation, needs, for someone else, etc…). Is the prayer an immediate need? An example of this would be, "Lord I am about to go into this interview, please help me with the appropriate words" or "Lord I was just in an accident, please let everyone involved be ok". I've been on my way into work before and noticed that the sunrise was beautiful. I have a small mountain that I cross on the way and I've stopped on that mountain and just thanked Him for that view. As you can see sitting in the morning having quiet time and speaking with Him is different than an immediate need but they are both valid forms of prayer. If you are praying for someone who is sick, your prayer maybe out loud but at home it may be silent. You might be kneeling at the altar or standing in the aisles. The important part of how-to is like the old Nike commercial says, "just do it". The more you do it the easier it will come. 1 Thessalonians 5:17 says, "pray without ceasing,".

As you begin praying, you might wonder about doing it 'right.' Jesus gives great advice just before the Lord's Prayer. You've probably heard its opening in Matthew 6:9 "Our Father in heaven, Hallowed be Your name." What most people miss is what comes before the Lord's Prayer. Matthew 6:5-8 gives advice on how to and how not to pray. Take a minute, type Matthew 6:5-8 in your phone or turn to it in your Bible and read the verses. Jesus is telling the disciples that your prayer is not to be done for others to hear so that you look more righteous. He's not saying don't pray out loud, especially if you are praying for someone else, but not to pray out loud for the purpose of being selfishly heard.

Just as the last chapter introduced the "SOAP" method for studying Scripture, a helpful guide for structuring your prayers is the "ACTS" method: A – Adoration, C – Confession, T – Thankfulness, S – Supplication.

A – Adoration

Begin your prayer with praise. Tell God who He is to you. Focus on His nature—His holiness, goodness, mercy, power, or love. You're not asking for anything yet; you're simply honoring Him.

"Lord, You are holy and faithful. You never change, and Your love never fails. I praise You because You are worthy of all glory."

C – Confession

Next, be honest about your shortcomings. Confess your sins to God in order to keep your relationship with Him open and healthy. He already knows, but He wants you to "use your words".

"Father, I confess my anger and impatience today. Forgive me for speaking harshly with my children. Cleanse my heart and help me walk in step with You."

T – Thanksgiving

Now thank God for what He's done. Be specific—thank Him for salvation, answered prayers, strength during trials, people in your life, or simple daily blessings.

"Thank You for the peace You gave me during that difficult meeting. Thank You for my family, for provision, and for never leaving me."

S – Supplication

Finally, bring your requests to God. This is where you ask Him to meet needs—yours or others'. It could be for healing, guidance, strength, provision, or anything else that weighs on your heart.

"Lord, please guide me in this decision I'm facing. I also lift up my friend who's struggling—give them comfort and direction."

This simple structure is to help you get started. Don't use it as some magic formula that you must do every time you pray. Want to know a secret? There are times when you will need to pray, but you will have absolutely no idea what to say. At times like these you have a helper who will step in and intercede for you. Romans 8:26 says, "Likewise the Spirit also helps in our weaknesses. For we do not know what we should pray for as we ought, but the Spirit Himself makes intercession for us with groanings which cannot be uttered." If you are at the end of your rope and the words won't come; sit, be still and quiet, let the Holy Spirit do His work.

Another point I would like to bring up about prayer is what we refer to as the "altar call". Many churches during their service will ask that anyone who needs prayer come down and kneel at the altar and speak with God about it. If you need prayer, go! A pastor (one I normally agree with) once said that we no longer have altars because the altar was a place of sacrifice and we no longer offer sacrifices, therefore, the altar call was unnecessary. I would like to strongly disagree with him. Romans 12:1 (NIV) says, "Therefore, I urge you, brothers and sisters,

41

in view of God's mercy, to *offer your bodies as a living sacrifice*, holy and pleasing to God—this is your true and proper worship." (emphasis mine). If you are in desperate need of prayer, by going down to the altar you are offering yourself as a living sacrifice which is pleasing to God. Don't be timid, don't be embarrassed, fight off the feeling that you shouldn't and go!

It can be tough starting a prayer life. Many people either don't have one at all or have very limited prayer time. Set aside a little time each day before or after your study time and just talk with Him.

As you grow in prayer and the Word, your understanding of core beliefs—your doctrine—will deepen. Let's explore that next.

Notes

Chapter 8

Doctrine: It's Important, But...

Ephesians 2:20

having been built on the foundation of the apostles and prophets, Jesus Christ Himself being the chief cornerstone,

To understand what doctrine is, we first need to define another word: theology. What is theology? Do a simple search online and you will get a wide range of answers. Dictionary.com says it's "the study of the nature of God and religious belief." Britannica.com goes a little bit further saying it's a, "philosophically oriented discipline of religious speculation and apologetics that is traditionally restricted, because of its origins and format, to Christianity but that may also encompass, because of its themes, other religions, including especially Islam and Judaism. The themes of theology include God, humanity, the world, salvation, and eschatology (the study of last times)". Huh? For this book, theology simply means the study of God.

That's theology. Now, what is doctrine? According to Dictionary.com, doctrine is "a belief or set of beliefs held and taught by a church, political party, or other group." The core beliefs you hold are your personal doctrines. Back in the Introduction, I mentioned that I hold to a Provisionist view of salvation (see Dr. Leighton Flowers' books[1] [2] in the Bibliography for more). That means my doctrine—my belief—on soteriology (a branch of theology that deals with salvation) is Provisionism.

As a new believer, studying God and His Word is important and your doctrine (set of beliefs) is important but it doesn't have to be formed all at once. Think of forming your doctrine like building a house. You don't start with the roof; you start with the foundation. You build a strong and sturdy foundation to hold up the rest of the house. Without a firm foundation, buildings crumble; the same is true for our beliefs.

As Paul mentions in Ephesians 2:20, Jesus is our chief Cornerstone. The cornerstone was normally the first stone laid down and all others were laid according to it. He also says that our foundation is the apostles and prophets.

So how do we build on the "foundation"? We read and study what the Cornerstone (Christ) and foundation (Apostles and Prophets) tell us. We read the Bible, study the Word, and listen to sound teaching and preaching. We slowly and methodically build our belief system one brick at a time. No one's doctrine is the same day one as it is year ten. We grow, learn, and begin to understand things that we could not before.

So, you know that you grow and learn, but what do I mean when I say "you could not understand before"? Exactly that! Before you were a believer you could not understand what the Bible says. Sure, you can read the words and understand them but the deeper meanings are hidden from non-believers. 1 Corinthians 2:14 (ESV) says, "The natural person does not accept the things of the Spirit of God, for they are folly to him, and he is not able to understand them because they are spiritually discerned." We as believers have the help of the Holy Spirit to understand the deeper meanings of the Bible. I will probably get pushback from non-believers because they can open the Bible and read the words, but try this, find a book on quantum physics and read it.

Here's an example from a book[3], written about wave-particle duality: "From the exponential fall-off of the radial distribution the binding energy was determined to be $151.9 \pm 13.3 \times 10^{-9}$ eV (1.5 ± 0.13 mK) with the highest precision so far. With the same apparatus in another remarkable experiment the radial distributions of the three helium atoms in the first excited Efimov state of helium trimer could also be measured". I can read every word in those two sentences, but I have absolutely no idea what they mean. I would need years of physics classes and instructors to be able to understand what is being said. It's the same for the Bible. There are scholars who have dedicated their entire lives to studying just one book, the Bible.

Not only do non-believers have a hard time understanding concepts in the Bible, but you will too. Even Peter had a hard time understanding some of what Paul wrote. He states in 2 Peter 3:15-16, "as also our beloved brother Paul, according to the wisdom given to him, has written to you, as also in all his epistles, speaking in them of these things, in which are some things hard to understand." As you read and study the

Bible don't get discouraged if at first there are "things hard to understand". That's true for everyone. Take your time, read from different versions, review commentaries but whatever you do, don't get discouraged. Stay in it.

The title of this chapter is "Doctrine: It's Important, But…" So what's the "But?" I once heard a pastor say "major on the majors and minor on the minors." What does that mean? It means there are essential doctrines to the Christian faith and there are non-essential doctrines. Essential doctrines are those that you must believe to be considered a Christian. Even these core beliefs will be debated by fringe groups but sound Christian groups will agree on them. An example of an essential belief is that Christ will return, when He will return is a non-essential belief. I fully believe that Christ will return and that He will return after a literal 7-year tribulation. His return is the essential part and the "literal 7-year tribulation" is the non-essential part. There is one essential truth about Christ's return—that He will return—and many non-essential views about when or how that will happen. The non-essential parts are fun to discuss and debate with fellow believers but don't get lost in them. For the first little while, spend your time laying the foundation of essentials before moving to the "minors".

In the next chapter we will tackle trying to avoid false doctrines, but I want to leave you with this quote, "In essentials, unity; in non-essentials, liberty; in all things, charity."[4] Barry's break down of this quote: we should unify around the essentials, we should give each other liberty in how we view the non-essentials, but in all of it we should be respectful of each other.

Notes

Notes

Chapter 9
Avoiding False Doctrine
Acts 20:29-30

For I know this, that after my departure savage wolves will come in among you, not sparing the flock. Also from among yourselves men will rise up, speaking perverse things, to draw away the disciples after themselves.

In Chapter 8, we discussed that doctrine is important, especially the essential doctrines, but that there is often leeway in the non-essential doctrines. If there is leeway for me to believe one way and you to believe another, what then is false doctrine? GotQuestions.org.[1] defines it this way, "False doctrine is any idea that adds to, takes away from, contradicts, or nullifies the doctrine given in God's Word." Let's return to the example from the last chapter: "Christ will return." In John 14:3 Jesus says, "And if I go and prepare a place for you, I will come again and receive you to Myself; that where I am, there you may be also." He clearly states that He will return to receive and take believers to be where He is. See also Matthew 24:36–44, Luke 21:25–28, John 5:28–29 among other Scriptures. Since this is clearly stated in Scripture, teaching that Christ will not return is false doctrine.

Another form of false doctrine is false prophecy. Above we saw Christ's return as essential doctrine; claiming a date for that return would be false prophecy. In Matthew 24, Jesus is teaching the disciples about the second coming and in verse 36 He states, "But of that day and hour no one knows, not even the angels of heaven, but My Father only." Jesus says that no one knows when it will happen, not even "the angels of heaven." Therefore, if you hear anyone give an exact date for His return, that is false prophecy. For example, in the 1840s, William Miller predicted Christ's return on October 22, 1844, based on his understanding of Daniel 8:14. When it didn't happen, his followers faced the 'Great Disappointment'.[2]

Mature believers enjoy discussing and debating non-essential doctrines. Try not to get caught up in these until you have laid a strong foundation like we discussed in Chapter 8.

The best way to avoid false doctrine is the way the Secret Service teaches its employees to spot counterfeit money. They have them study the real thing until they can spot it in their sleep. There are so many different ways to counterfeit money that it would be impossible to study them all, but if you know the real thing inside and out, you can spot counterfeit bills immediately. Like the false teachings we've discussed, the same goes for doctrine: study the Bible and know it inside and out, and you can spot counterfeit doctrine the same way. 2 Timothy 3:16–17 says, "All Scripture is given by inspiration of God, and is profitable for doctrine, for reproof, for correction, for instruction in righteousness, that the man of God may be complete, thoroughly equipped for every good work." If you stay in the Word, you will be able to see false doctrine from a mile away. If you've followed the advice in Chapter 3 and found a good solid church, talk with your church leadership, your small group leader, or a grounded friend about any new doctrine you hear. They can help you ensure the doctrine aligns with Scripture's clear teachings.

Please take this next piece of advice to heart: initially, while you are still new to the faith, avoid all television and YouTube preachers. There are so many of these who teach false doctrines and do it so skillfully that it becomes almost impossible to tell the good from the bad, unless you are well grounded and solid on your foundation. Early on in my walk, I began a verse-by-verse study. It was awesome. The teacher explained things so simply that even I could understand them. He had a 30-minute show on TV in the mornings and I would sit with my Bible and follow right along. I even purchased the exact same version of the Bible he was teaching from. Slowly but surely, I wandered off into a doctrine that I look back on now, and can't believe I bought into it. The doctrine is called Ultra- or Hyper-Dispensationalism, which divides Scripture in extreme ways. Explaining why it's wrong is a topic for another book on another day, but if you're curious, you can look it up online.

There are some really good and really bad resources out there. Research your research sources. I know that sounds funny, but it's true. Every resource has some bias, including me. They may try to be unbiased but in some ways their bias will come through. That is why I started this book the way I did in the introduction. I wanted you to know up front what my biases are. I have tried to write this book from as neutral of a position as my beliefs will allow but I am quite positive that some of my own biases have shown through. Listed on the bibliography page for chapter 6 is a list of resources I use. If you decide to use any of these resources keep the following things in mind:

- I'm not Paul–trust but verify these resources yourself.
- Just because you use a resource for study does not mean you have to agree with everything they teach.
- Consider the depth of the resource–are you ready for it yet?
- The number one resource is the Bible itself.

Another tool to use against false teaching is a firm grip on the truth—and the clearest truth you have is what God has done in your own life. Doctrine matters, but so does your personal testimony. In the next chapter, we'll talk about your story—how God saved you, changed you, and how He might use that story to reach someone else. Be ready to share it.

Notes

Notes

Chapter 10
Be Ready with Your Story
Luke 8:39

Return to your own house, and tell what great things God has done for you." And he went his way and proclaimed throughout the whole city what great things Jesus had done for him.

I was raised in a "Christian" home. We went to church occasionally, and if you had asked me, I would have said yes, I am a Christian. That would be the same answer I would give for many years. Now, jump forward to 2004. When my wife and I began discussing marriage, one of the things she wanted was for us to find a church we both liked. After marrying, we built a home and started looking for churches. After visiting several churches, we found one that we both liked, and joined. In 2007 our pastor challenged the congregation to give two percent of their time to mission work. He said, if you are willing to commit to that, come down front. I was not willing; however, my wife was, and down front she went. A few weeks later, she let me know that she was going to Venezuela for a week on a mission trip. Being a male of the species, I was not going to let my bride go out of the country without me there to protect her. So, the last week of 2007, we flew to Maracaibo, Venezuela, for a medical mission trip. There were two teams: the medical team and the entertainment. We were the entertainment. We would put on a "carnival" while children were waiting to see the doctors. Just for this trip I learned how to tie balloon animals to give the children. These children had nothing. Their clothes were rags, houses were ramshackle, and meals came sporadically. Their parents quite literally competed with each other at the local dump for whatever useful items they could find. The one thing I noticed was that all of the kids had this joy about them. They had nothing, yet I watched as older children would give younger children items first. To the best of my memory, I don't recall one of those children saying "mine," and trying to keep something to themselves. As the week progressed, my heart was pulled harder and harder until New Year's Eve. We were leaving the next day, so we went back to the hotel earlier than normal. We packed and prepared to leave the next morning. That night I could not sleep. I tossed and turned until finally about 2 a.m. I rolled out of bed, hit my knees, and surrendered my life to Christ. My wife heard me crying, and asked what the problem was. I told her I had just been saved. I will never forget her response, "It's about time." She had known the whole time, but I had not. There was a staff member from the church with us, and he and I discussed what had happened. The staff member discipled me over the next few months, and I was baptized.

That's it—that's my story.

No big turn from drugs or alcohol. No paralyzing light from above—just plain old heartstrings being played by a master musician. You see, I had spent years thinking I was a Christian. I knew there was a God, and I knew His Son had been real but I had never acknowledged Him as the Lord of my life. I had been doing exactly the opposite of Proverbs 3:5. It says, "Trust in the Lord with all your heart, And lean not on your own understanding;". Once I did trust in Him with all my heart verse 6 came to life for me. It says, "In all your ways acknowledge Him, And He shall direct your paths." He has been directing the path of my life ever since.

Now, what is your story? Your story is your "testimony". It testifies to others what God has done for you. People mistakenly think that you have to be this great evangelistic speaker to bring people to Christ. When in actuality people just need to see and hear what God has done in your life. So be ready with that story.

Take some time to write a few things down while they're still fresh. You don't have to write the whole story, but jot down things like dates, people involved, key moments, or anything that helps bring those memories back. Most of all, do not be ashamed of your story. It is your story of salvation, it is important. Luke 15:7 says, "I say to you that likewise there will be more joy in heaven over one sinner who repents than over ninety-nine just persons who need no repentance." And 3 verses later Luke 15:10 says, "Likewise, I say to you, there is joy in the presence of the angels of God over one sinner who repents." If you were saved out of something you were ashamed of, that shame has been removed, be proud that it is gone. If your story, like mine, was just a simple story—don't be ashamed, it will affect someone when they hear it.

We saw in the chapter on change, to not judge your change against other's change. Don't judge your testimony against someone else's testimony. Your testimony is yours for a reason. It was given to you for the purpose of sharing with someone who needs it. The problem is, you don't know who that person is! God knows, that's why He gave it to you, so share it with everyone who will listen because they may be the person it was intended for.

We've stepped through many thoughts and ideas to get to this point. Let's wrap it all up in the next chapter, "Where do I go from here?"

Notes

Notes

Chapter 11

Where Do I Go from Here

Philippians 1:6

Being confident of this very thing, that He who has begun a good work in you will complete it until the day of Jesus Christ.

You've made it to the end of this book—but really, you're just getting started. If you've accepted Jesus as your Lord and Savior, then you're not who you used to be. Whether it felt dramatic or quiet, something truly eternal has happened in you. And now, you may be wondering: what do I do next?

That's what this final chapter is about—where do I go from here.

Keep Growing

Salvation is the beginning of a new life, not the end of a to-do list. God didn't just save you from something—He saved you for something. You're now part of His plan, His family, and His purpose.

Don't worry about becoming a spiritual giant overnight. Growth is a process. The Holy Spirit will lead you step by step. But you must play your part. In his book *The Joy of Preaching*,[1] Phillips Brooks says, "We will never become truly spiritual by sitting down and wishing to become so."

You grow by doing the things we've talked about:
- Regularly reading and studying the Bible
- Praying and talking to God
- Staying connected to a healthy church
- Watching out for false teaching
- Telling your story
- Asking questions and learning sound doctrine

You don't have to master all of this at once. Just stay faithful in the little things, and over time, you'll look back and be amazed at what God has done.

Get Plugged In

If you haven't already found a church, make that a top priority. You weren't meant to do this alone. The Christian life is personal, but it's not private. You need other believers—and they need you, too.

Look for a church that teaches the Bible clearly, worships Jesus boldly, and makes space for you to grow. Be open to serving, even if you're new. You might not be teaching a class yet, but you can hold a door, help in the kitchen, or greet someone with a smile. Those small acts matter more than you think.

And if you've already found a church, plant yourself there. Stay through the awkward weeks and don't let little differences turn you away. Give it time. Real growth happens when we stick around long enough to grow roots.

Stay Humble and Curious

You don't have to have all the answers. In fact, the moment you think you do, you're probably heading into dangerous territory. Be a lifelong learner. The Bible is deep—you won't exhaust it. Doctrine takes time to develop. Your understanding will grow and mature the more time you spend with God and His Word.

Ask questions. Be curious. Just be sure you're getting your answers from trustworthy sources—Scripture first, then wise, biblically grounded teachers. And when you don't know something, be honest. "I'm still learning" is a perfectly good answer.

If you ever feel stuck or unsure, don't forget the invitation God gives in James 1:5: "If any of you lacks wisdom, let him ask of God, who gives to all liberally and without reproach, and it will be given to him."

He's not holding back. He wants to give you wisdom as you seek Him.

Deal with Doubt the Right Way

Every believer wrestles with doubt at some point. You might go through a season where God feels distant, or where something in the Bible doesn't make sense yet. That's normal.

The key isn't to hide it—it's to bring it into the light. Talk to a mature believer. Pray about it. Search the Scriptures. Doubt isn't the enemy of faith; staying stuck in it is. Don't let momentary confusion lead you to walk away from what you know is true. God is patient. He's not threatened by your questions.

Keep Your Eyes on Jesus

There's going to be a lot coming at you—opinions, expectations, even well-meaning advice. Keep your focus on Jesus. He's the center of it all. He's your Savior, your example, your foundation. Keep reading the Gospels. Pay attention to how He treated people, how He prayed, how He loved.

When you don't know what to do next, ask, "What would Jesus have me do?" That's a better compass than most voices you'll hear.

I once heard a pastor say, "When you don't know what to do next, keep doing the last thing God had you do until He tells you something else." That's stuck with me. So if you're unsure what comes next, maybe that's God telling you to stay where you are a little longer. Just be ready for the next thing when it comes.

Be Ready to Share What You've Found

As you grow, you'll find people around you start to notice. They may not say it, but they'll sense something different—and if they ask, be ready with your story.

Peter writes in 1 Peter 3:15, "Always be ready to give a defense to everyone who asks you a reason for the hope that is in you, with meekness and fear."

You don't have to be a preacher or a theologian to make a difference. You just have to be willing to share what He did for you. God loves to work through ordinary people—let Him.

You Won't Always Feel It—That's Okay

There will be days where you feel on fire for God, and there will be days where you feel cold or confused. Faith is not always a feeling. It's trust. Trust that God is still with you. Trust that He's still working, even when you can't see it. Trust that the good work He began in you— He will complete.

Before We Part

If I could sit across the table from you, I'd simply say: stay close to Jesus, stay in His Word, stay connected to His people. The rest will come.

There's still so much ahead of you. This new life you've started isn't a finish line—it's a starting line. Build on your foundation with truth, prayer, fellowship, and love. Don't be afraid to trip. Just get back up and keep moving forward.

And remember, you're not walking alone—He promises to be with you every step of the way.

Matthew 28: 18-20

And Jesus came and spoke to them, saying, "All authority has been given to Me in heaven and on earth. Go therefore and make disciples of all the nations, baptizing them in the name of the Father and of the Son and of the Holy Spirit, teaching them to observe all things that I have commanded you; and lo, I am with you always, even to the end of the age." Amen.

Notes

Bibliography

Introduction
1. Sproul, R. C. Essential Truths of the Christian Faith. Tyndale House Publishers, 1992.

Chapter 1: First Question
1. Got Questions Ministries. 'What Is Repentance and Is It Necessary for Salvation?' GotQuestions.org. Accessed April 22, 2025. https://www.gotquestions.org/repentance-salvation.html.
2. Henry, Matthew. *Concise Commentary on the Whole Bible*. London, 1706. Digitized by BibleHub. Accessed April 22, 2025. https://biblehub.com/commentaries/mhc/.

Chapter 2: What has Changed
1. Walsh, Joe. 'Life's Been Good.' Recorded on *But Seriously, Folks....* Asylum Records, 1978.

Chapter 3: Find a Good Church
1. Davidson, Karen Lynn, Whittaker, David J., Ashurst-McGee, Mark; Jensen, Richard L., eds. (2012). "Historical Introduction to 'Church History,' 1 March 1842". Joseph Smith Histories, 1832–1844. The Joseph Smith Papers: Histories. Vol. 1. Church Historian's Press. pp. 489–501.
2. Voorhees, Amy B. 'Christian Science.' In *The Cambridge Companion to Mary Baker Eddy,*

edited by Paul C. Gutjahr, 45. Cambridge: Cambridge University Press, 2008.
3. Church Locators
    a. Southern Baptist Church Finder

    b. Church.org

    c. Calvary Chapel Church Finder

    d. Evangelical Free Church Finder

    e. IFCA Church Finder

Chapter 4: Baptism

1. Got Questions Ministries. 'What Is the Importance of Christian Baptism?' GotQuestions.org. Accessed April 28, 2025. https://www.gotquestions.org/Christian-baptism.html.

2. Ready to Harvest – YouTube Channel providing denominational overviews and church history insights. https://www.youtube.com/@ReadyToHarvest

3. Grudem, Wayne. Systematic Theology: An Introduction to Biblical Doctrine. 2nd ed. Grand Rapids: Zondervan Academic, 2020. Pg 1196

4. Sproul, R. C. Essential Truths of the Christian Faith. Tyndale House Publishers, 1992. Pg290

Chapter 5: How to Choose a Bible

1. Winger, Mike. 'The best Bible Version May Depend on Your Education Level.' YouTube video June 2, 2021 https://www.youtube.com/watch?v=lykAMFbbfsI

2. Recommended Resources
   a. How to Choose a Bible Version: Making Sense of the Bible Marketplace by Robert L. Thomas
   b. Mike Winger. YouTube video, "Can I trust Bible Translations: evidence for the Bible pt17": November 11, 2016
   c. The Biblical Roots Podcast YouTube video "which English translation is best?" May 1, 2023

Chapter 6: How to Study the Bible
1. Study resources
   a. Bible Gateway – https://biblegateway.com/
   I use this site almost daily. You can open the Bible in many different versions and compare versions side by side.
   b. Bible Hub - https://biblehub.com/
   I use this site when I'm preparing a lesson for Sunday school. It gives you access to different commentaries, versions, Greek info, etc.
   c. Got Questions - https://gotquestions.org/
   Got Questions gives good solid answers to biblical questions, according to the website today, there are 9,782 articles.
   d. Pastor Mike Winger - https://biblethinker.org/ and
      https://www.youtube.com/@MikeWinger
   In all honesty I have never used his website but I have spent many hours on his YouTube channel. He has a hodgepodge of content from verse-by-verse studies to question and answer sessions to stand alone videos on specific subjects.

2. Pastors that I trust. These are pastors that I trust and will listen to their sermons and teachings but I know each of their theologies and so take certain areas of their teachings with a grain of salt. Remember just because I disagree with one part of their theology doesn't mean I can't learn from them.
   A. Pastor Rick Wright – The Church at Chelsea-Westover (my church)

B. Pastor Danny Lovett – Jesus is Awesome Ministries
C. Pastor Louie Giglio – Passion City Church
D. Pastor Matt Chandler – Village Church
E. Pastor Leighton Flowers – Trinity Seminary
F. Pastor David Guzik – Enduring Word Ministries
G. Pastor Paul LeBoutillier – Calvary Chapel Ontario
H. Pastor Alistair Begg – Parkside Church
I. The Late Pastor Stephen Armstrong – Verse by Verse Ministry International

Chapter 7: Prayer

This chapter reflects personal practice and biblical encouragement; no outside sources cited.

Chapter 8: Doctrine: It's Important, But…

1. Flowers, Leighton. God's Provision for All: A Defense of God's Goodness. Independently Published, 2020.
2. Flowers, Leighton. The Potter's Promise: A Biblical Defense of Traditional Soteriology. Trinity Academic Press, 2017.
3. Toennies, J. Peter. 'Otto Stern and Wave-Particle Duality.' In *Molecular Beams in Physics and Chemistry*, edited by Bretislav Friedrich and Horst Schmidt-Böcking. Cham: Springer, 2021.
4. Meldenius, Rupertus. Paraenesis votiva pro Pace Ecclesiae ad Theologos Augustanae Confessionis. Rottenberg: Hieronymus Körnlein, 1626. Earlier use attributed to Marco Antonio de Dominis, De Repubblica Ecclesiastica, 1617.

Chapter 9: Avoiding False Doctrine
1. Got Questions Ministries. 'What is false doctrine?' GotQuestions.org Accessed May 1, 2025.
https://www.gotquestions.org/false-doctrine.html

2. Knight, George R. Millennial Fever and the End of the World: A Study of Millerite Adventism. Boise: Pacific Press, 1993.

Chapter 10: Be ready with your story
Based on the author's personal testimony and Scripture.

Chapter 11: Where Do I Go from Here?
1. Brooks, Phillips. "The Joy of Preaching". New York: Dodd, Mead and Company, 1899.